Meet the Minibeasts

Contents   **Page**

written by Rachel Walker

Minibeasts is the collective name we give to small spineless creatures, also known as invertebrates – animals with no backbone. When scientists called zoologists study animals, Minibeasts are much easier to study than other animal groups like vertebrates. Imagine catching a tiger to learn about its features! A snail or fly must be much easier to handle! Minibeasts range in size from the tiniest mite to the much larger octopus and lobster.

There are 5 major groups of Minibeasts:
1. Insects, which have 6 legs and 3 body parts.
2. Arachnids with 8 legs.
3. Crustaceans, which have hard shells and many legs.
4. Myriapods with 10-200 legs.
5. Mollusks or Gastropods, which have no legs.

Habitat

There are millions of Minibeasts living all over the Earth, and some live in the sea, too. They live almost everywhere – in trees, in water, on the ground and underground – some even share our homes! They are in fields and forests, on farms and in gardens. Different species live where they can jump, crawl, fly, swim, dive or walk on water. Some types, like ticks and fleas, are even found living on other animals!

Minibeasts are an essential part of the Earth's eco-system and the food chain because they are a food source for many creatures such as reptiles, birds and fish, as well as for mammals and even humans. Some species are useful recyclers of waste material, and some do vital work pollinating plants as they move from flower to flower. The plants then provide food for animals and humans.

What is an insect?

Insects are the biggest group, by far, of all Minibeasts – there are more than a million different types of insects (that we know about) living on Earth. They are studied by scientists called entomologists, who record facts about this major group of Minibeasts. All insects have six legs. The skeleton is on the outside of the body. This is called an exoskeleton, and it protects the insect's organs.

An insect's body is made up of 3 regions:

1. Head
2. Thorax
3. Abdomen.

The head has 6 segments fused together – a set of mouthparts, a pair of compound eyes, and a pair of antennae used for smelling and tasting. Antennae are often called feelers because that is exactly what they do: touch, taste and feel. Compound eyes are covered with thousands of tiny lenses: e.g. A fly has about 4,000 lenses in one eye! This means insects have excellent eyesight. Humans don't have compound eyes: we have only one lens in each eye.

The thorax is the middle section of the insect's body and is made up
of three segments. Insects have six legs attached to their thorax.
These legs are made up of jointed segments and have claws. Some
insects have wings, and these are attached to their thorax, too. The
wings are folded when the insects are not flying.

The abdomen is the lower section divided into eleven segments, but not all of these are visible. Well-protected by the exoskeleton, the insect's abdomen contains essential organs like the respiratory system, digestive system, the heart and the reproductive system.

Arachnids

There are about 60,000 species of Arachnids, including spiders, scorpions, mites and ticks. Arachnids are usually predators that eat insects and other creatures, so they must hunt for their food. Scorpions have killer stinging tails and pincers. Spiders spin webs to help them trap and catch their prey. Arachnids often kill their prey with their poisonous fangs and then inject it with digestive juices to dissolve the flesh before sucking it up.

All arachnids have:
- Two parts to their body
- Eight legs
- A hard exoskeleton
- A pair of either pincers or fangs.

They don't have wings or antennae. Most have eight eyes. The two body parts are the cephalothorax and the abdomen. The cephalothorax contains the legs, mouthparts and sense organs. The abdomen contains the respiratory system, digestive system, reproductive system and the heart.

aggressive scorpion

Crustaceans

Most of this group of
Minibeasts live in water.
Lice, crabs, shrimps,
barnacles and lobsters
are all crustaceans.
Other features are:
- 2 pairs of antennae
- Fan-shaped tail
- Many pairs of
  jointed legs
- Egg-laying
- No wings
- Farmed or collected
  for food.

They have a hard
exoskeleton or "crust"
that they outgrow and
then replace (by growing
a new one).

crab laying eggs

Myriapods

Myriapods are remarkable for their number of legs – they can
have between 10 and 200 pairs of legs!
Centipedes and millipedes are Myriapods.

- The name Myriapod means "lots of legs".
- Most live in dark, damp places.
- Some Myriapods are so tiny you need a microscope to see
  them, but some are as long as your forearm!

Centipedes have many segments to their body, and each segment has one pair of legs attached to it. Millipedes have two pairs of legs on each body segment. Centipedes are predators, but millipedes are vegetarians.

Mollusks or Gastropods are Minibeasts that don't have any legs. Instead they have a muscle that acts like a foot. Snails, shellfish, octopuses and slugs are all mollusks. Many mollusks live in fresh water or the sea, and some have shells, but none have wings.

Another group of Minibeasts, Annelids, includes soft-bodied creatures like worms and leeches. Earthworms live underground, where they do vital work improving the soil and supporting plant growth.

Life cycles

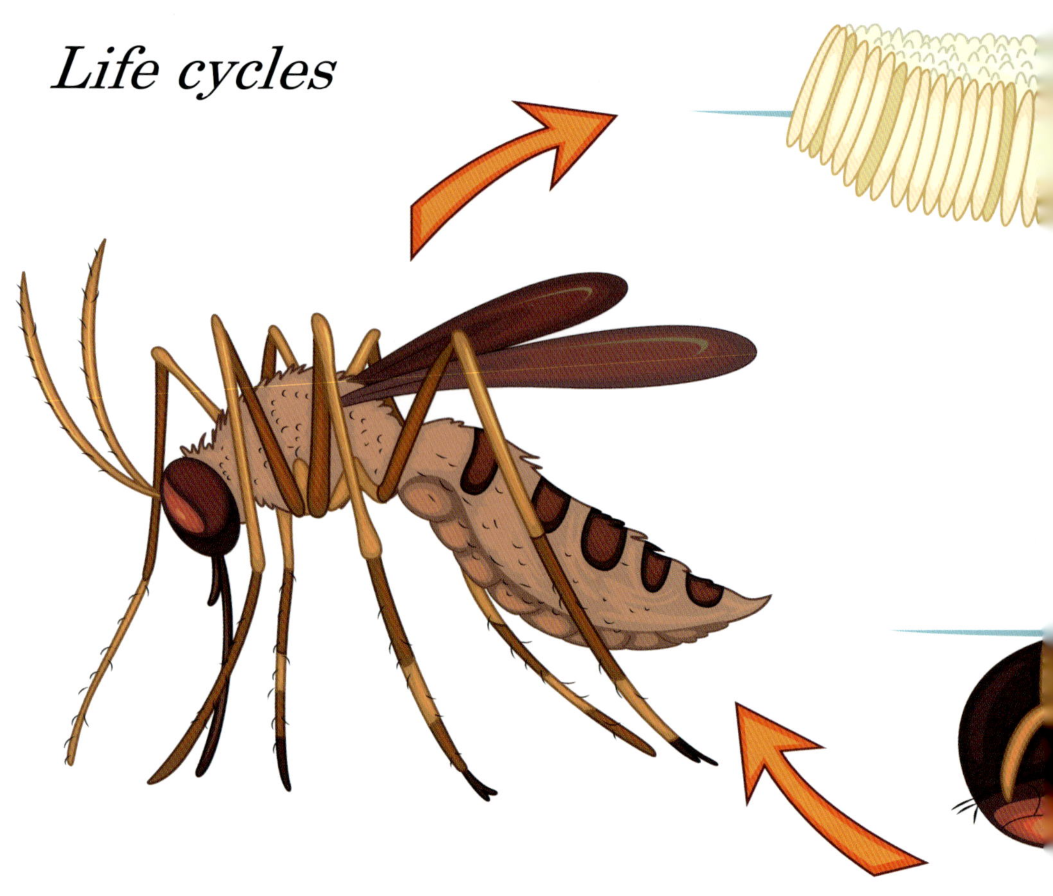

The life cycle of a mosquito is very similar to that of most insects: i.e. egg to larva to pupa to adult.

The mosquito lays up to 400 eggs on or near water. The eggs hatch out to larvae (known as "wrigglers"), which feed on tiny particles in the water. As the larva grows, it sheds its skin four times, then changes into the pupa (also called a "tumbler"). Inside the pupa's case, the insect develops the organs and structures of a mature mosquito.

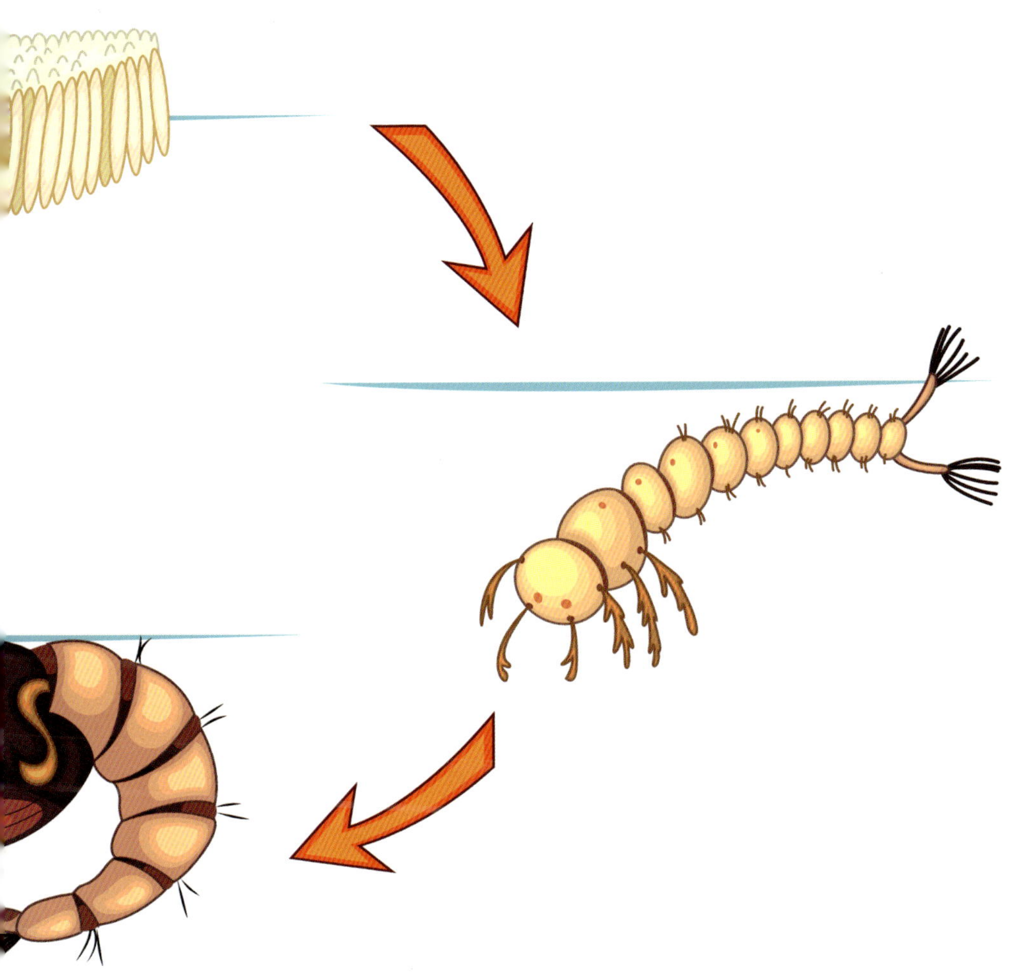

When it is ready to emerge, the adult mosquito splits the pupal case and rests on the surface of the water to dry and harden. In warm weather the whole life cycle can be completed in 1-2 weeks, when the new mosquitoes are ready to immediately start the cycle of development turning again.

No wonder the Minibeasts' group forms an enormous part of the world's animal life!